FORGIVENESS ISN'T FOR PUSSIES

No bullshit advice on how to get past infidelity,
and get your relationship back.
(Without feeling like a crazy person.)

FORGIVENESS

is **not** a sign of weakness

FORGIVENESS

is **not** old-fashioned

LOVE

is **not** dead

HOPE

is **not** lost

FORGIVENESS

is a choice

FORGIVENESS

takes hard work

LOVE

is real

HOPE

is something to cling to

DEDICATION

To my partner in life. You have taught me absolutely everything I know about forgiveness. You faced with process with humility and love and I honestly can't imagine what my life would've been like without you.
Thank you for owning your imperfections.
Thank you for choosing our family.
Thank you for walking through the fire with me.
And finally, thank you for letting me speak my truth.
I love you, punk.

And to the other loves of my life; Em and Fisch. You have made me a believer in unconditional love. You made me softer and able to appreciate vulnerability. Being your Mom is the biggest gift. Let this book not diminish the awesome thoughts you have of your Dad, but instead, I hope this multiplies them. People make mistakes, and I cannot protect you from hurt. I will, hopefully, teach you resiliency and how to forgive. And seek forgiveness. Your Daddy and I did the work. Both for us, and for you. Messing up is hard. Making it right is even harder.
But it's so worth it.
We love you to the ends of the universe.

CONTENTS

START HERE
1. MY PERSONAL MESS
2. GROUND RULES
3. RULES MANAGING THOSE DAMN EXPECTATIONS

IN THE TRENCHES
4. DIRTY TRUTHS
5. LOOSE LIPS
6. HOT TOPICS
7. TRIGGERS
8. SETTLING THE SCORE

MOVING FORWARD
9. RENEGOTIATION CONTRACT
10. OPPORTUNITIES TO SUCCEED
11. REIGNITING THAT FLAME
12. SO...NOW WHAT?

1 MY PERSONAL MESS

It was 2012, late January, I was eight months pregnant with our hard-tried-for second child, and we had just showed up for duty at Conrad's new position at the Coast Guard station in Panama City Beach, Florida. I had traveled there with our toddler months beforehand, finding us the most amazing hundred-year-old farm house. It was bright red with white trim, with a massive magnolia tree on one side, and a large oak on the other, shading most of the front of the house. It was like something out of a storybook, down to its squeaky floors. We had just closed escrow and gotten the keys. We were settling in, I was in full nesting mode. There wasn't a room that I didn't paint. There wasn't a crib or bouncer that could wait to be assembled.

One morning, I remember my husband calling to check in on me. I missed his call because I was precariously perched on our kitchen counter while reaching to paint a missed spot behind the cabinets. My degree is in Interior Design, so there wasn't a single space safe from me.

Exhausted from stocking the nursery, I decided to take a break while Emma napped. I sat down in my oversized leather chair. A chair that I have always loved, but there was something almost intoxicating about that level of comfort my body experienced while sitting my swollen, pregnant body in it.

I opened the laptop to check my email and probably do some last minute online baby purchases when I noticed an unusual email in my inbox; from our cell phone carrier. Now, I have been with the same company for years, even before I knew my husband. And by this point, we'd had the same plan for years, and it was on auto-pay.
We rarely received notices. Of any kind.
So, this caught my attention.

I don't recall the exact wording of the subject line, but it went something along the lines of,

"We are contacting you regarding the unusual spike in usage on your account. You have $XXX in overage charges."

Instantly, my heart sank into the pit of my very large stomach.

Not because I am a typically pessimistic person. Actually, some might call me annoyingly optimistic. I am a people-pleaser, and consider myself pretty polite, as such, I generally get the better side of people in our interactions. My world view of the human race is overwhelming positive with a few bad seeds.

Not because I am untrusting.

I wish I could say this was the first time I had dealt with cheating in a relationship, but who are we kidding? But even that didn't make me swear off the idea of monogamy all together. In fact, I met my husband shortly after ending a long relationship over the guy cheating. But I firmly believe in not holding someone accountable for another's mistakes.

Not because I was suspicious to begin with. I was full of emotions... I mean, hormones. I joke, but that's serious. I was elated about the pregnancy, and the house, and be married. I was into it. I liked playing house.

There was no initial reason for me to think the worse.

But I did. And turns out,
I was right.

That was 6 years ago. (At the time I write this.)

We are still married.
We got through it.
And we got our happy back.

Ok, we are really good. But we aren't perfect. Not separately, or as a couple. We still have fights that hit more below the belt then they should. We still disagree over the kids and we still lose our shit from time to time.

But what makes our mess different, is our open communication. And possibly, our commitment to each other. We have proven to each other that we aren't going to just throw in the towel when things get tough.

That's when real growth happens.

We have a level of self-awareness that neither of us had before. It's a new level of intense to view yourself through your partner's eyes. Especially when you're in the midst of crisis.

Honestly, this was the hardest thing that I have ever gone through. I would venture to say that it was even harder than a serious medical event we went through with one of our children. At least for that, we had each other. And a lot of outside support.

Going through something like this in a relationship brings up all those nasty demons that we try so hard to keep hidden. Things inside ourselves, our partner, and in humanity in general. Things that just aren't talked about because the level of shame that accompanies this type of action.

But grieving after infidelity, is emotional distress that is done mostly behind doors. Alone.

We really had no idea how to move forward, I just knew we had to. So we basically pieced together ideas on how to get through this. We took some advice from therapists, some from trusted books, and the few people we confided in. I was a stay at home Mom, so nap times were spend scouring the internet for resources on how to get through this.

Want to know what I didn't find much of?

Couples that had openly walked in our shoes.

There were resources on how to be independent and leave your partner, that just didn't appeal to me. And then there are the religious guides for staying, but they are basically breaking it down to staying for the sake of not getting divorced.
Neither of those applied to us.

I needed logic.
I needed a guide.
I couldn't just pray my way through this.

See, the thing is, I do believe in God, and in prayer. I have seen first hand what prayer can do for someone. But in those first few days, and weeks after I found out about the affair, it became so abundantly clear that I was going to need something more tangible. I like to be in control of things, and I needed something to *do.*

Prayer wasn't going to save my marriage. So we figured it out ourselves.

My husband and I saved our marriage.

Logic saved our marriage.

Honest conversations saved our marriage.

Hard work saved our marriage.

2 GROUND RULES

This book is not a promise that you and your will live happily ever after. That's a fucking fairytale.

I'm not a therapist and this isn't *that book* on cheating.

Consider me your friend. Giving it to you straight.

I will give you logical advice, and practical, tangible things that you can *actually do*, based partially on my personal story, and part based on good 'ol research.

This book is really about forgiveness.

(That you can use in all aspects of your life, but obviously is geared toward this particular topic of infidelity.)

Because sometimes, bad s**t happens to good people.

But seriously, were you ever taught **how** to forgive?

We learn that we *need* to forgive.

Forgiveness isn't for Pussies

But *how*, exactly, isn't something I was taught.

What even *is* forgiveness? And what does it look like? What does it feel like?

Yeah, I didn't know either.

For the majority of us, forgiveness up until this point, has most likely been pretty mild. Forgiving Becky for going on a date with Ashton when she knew I liked him. Or forgiving my sister for constantly stealing my clothes. (Or was that the other way around?) Or seeking forgiveness from our parents for making stupid teenage decisions. We've likely all been there.

But there are a couple differences with those scenarios and what we are facing here; the stakes are high and the emotions are higher.

Were you *really* that sorry for missing curfew?
Did you feel *that* badly about going on a fun date with
    a cute guy? Who wasn't even into your friend?

The answer is most likely, no.

The situation seemed trivial. Mostly because, it was.

Fast forward to the current situation. And the shit is for real: nothing trivial about it. There are deep, dark, gnarly emotions and important relationships on the line. These are major life messes; with financial, emotional, and sometimes legal ramifications.
Yeah, nothing trivial about that scenario.

So, let the learning begin.

Learning (yes, learning) how to forgive.

Forgiveness doesn't just magically *happen* over time.
Although that would be super awesome.

Resentment happens over time.
Bitterness happens over time.

Forgiveness is a choice.

And a damn hard one.

You are choosing to walk through the fire,
instead of away from it.

That is some heavy sh**t.
Don't diminish the gravity of that.

While in traditional therapy, there was something about forgiveness that our counselor said that just stuck with me.
It's something that I suggest you read, and re-read, maybe even write it somewhere where you can read it, if you think that might be helpful.

> "Not forgiving, is like drinking poison and expecting the other person to die."

A quick internet search and you will find endless resources for scientific research that proves how strongly our emotions can effect our health; both physical and mental. Holding a grudge, or not putting in effort to forgive can literally make you sick. Not to mention, crazy.

John Hopkins is one of many great sources on the subject. Karen Swartz, M.D., director of the Mood Disorders Adult Consultation Clinic at The Johns Hopkins Hospital has written some things worth quoting.

> "There is an enormous physical burden to being hurt and disappointed." K. Swartz M.D.
>
> Chronic anger puts you into a fight-or-flight mode, which results in numerous changes in heart rate, blood pressure and immune response. Those changes, then, increase the risk of depression, heart disease and diabetes, among other conditions. Forgiveness, however, calms stress levels, leading to improved health.
>
> "It is an active process in which you make a conscious decision to let go of negative feelings whether the person deserves it or not," Swartz says. As you release the anger, resentment and hostility, you begin to feel empathy, compassion and sometimes even affection for the person who wronged you.
>
> (John Hopkins Medicine, Forgiveness: Your Health Depends on It)

While this book was written to specifically help you through forgiving your partner after infidelity, ultimately, your act of forgiveness isn't for *them*.

It's for **you.**

If you can end up happily ever after, together and committed, that's my most desired outcome.

I'm a romantic. I believe in love. I believe in creating long lasting relationships. I believe that if you really love someone, you have to love the 'bad' parts of them as well.

But there is a change that you may not end up together. There is a change that that might actually be the best outcome, in your situation. *Because ultimately, I think we all deserve happiness, and ultimately, learning how to forgive is at the root, about finding happiness.*

Regardless of the outcome of this particular situation that you are going through, hopefully reading this book, and going through the steps with your partner will leave you with something incredibly valuable;

Releasing the burden of holding a grudge.

Holding a grudge is heavy. Like turn you into a person you don't want to be- heavy. Hopefully this book helps give you the tools to put that demon to bed.

Because let's face it, forgiveness sounds really great in theory, but it can also seem like climbing Everest.

So, may I present to you my gift; the cheat sheet to forgiveness.

In all seriousness, if you do the work, whatever the outcome of your relationship, you will hopefully find forgiveness and even some empowerment.

> **Empowerment**
> In your decisions
> In your resiliency
> In your ability to overcome
> In your ability to love again

3 MANAGING THOSE DAMN EXPECTATIONS

No, I'm not insulting your intelligence.

But I do feel as though we need a disclaimer here.

Let's just cut to the chase....

Not all relationships are worth saving.

Ok, that's not exactly breaking news, but it also isn't really covered in most self-help books for overcoming infidelity.

But this isn't one of *those* self-help books.
Not to sound snarky.
If you are a person of science, and believe in logic and rational thinking, then you already know the above statement is true.

What you may not know is; if you qualify.

Simply,

Is my relationship worth saving?

It's very easy, especially those of us in long-term relationships, to just start *dialing it in*.

Until an issue like this arises, you may have been naively thinking that your relationship is okay.
* I use the word naive, not as an insult, but more in the sense of being optimistically unaware.

For some of us, we thought our relationships were more than okay. Others, may have had a little inkling that things were brewing under the surface.

Regardless of the relationship status before the news broke, as you move through this book, and the aftermath of the affair, it will become clear about what kind of relationship, and connection you *do have.*

And hopefully this will provide a way to make it better.

SO, WHAT DO YOU DO FIRST?

Personally, my initial reaction was to give his ass the boot. No, you can't live here. No, you won't be holding my hand when I give birth. No, you can't still have me as your wife after you've done some shit like this!

I come from a long line of matriarchs; strong, independent women that wouldn't tolerate being mistreated by anyone. Certainly not from within the family. Which only strengthens my stance on telling my husband to find somewhere else to live.

Survey says; that's probably how most of you reacted.

But here's the thing; that are you actually *gaining* in this decision? What can actually get better from separation?

One argument would be that everyone needs 'space' to cool off. And I get that. That's what I thought I wanted.

And what I told him I wanted.

I yelled. But I was also 8 months pregnant and wanted to stay calm for the baby. If I hadn't, who knows what would've happened?

But when I had gotten my grievances out, and my blood pressure began going back to healthy levels, I had this wave of emotion.

Have you ever experienced buyer's remorse before you even buy it? Let's say you are at Nordstrom, and you've really been wanting this pair of Gucci sunglasses. You technically have the money, but really have no business spending it on a new pair of sunnies. You hold said items in your hand as you browse the handbag section and even though you really, really want these bad-boys, you start feeling guilty about your purchase before you even have the cashier ring you up? Ever had that happen? Just me?
Well, that's the best way to describe what came over me.
That and the fact that even after my hurt-fueled insult brigade was over, my husband refused to leave.

Not in an aggressive, "you (physically) cant make me leave" type of way, but more like a "you cant make me leave, please don't make me leave."

He was literally on his knees in our garden. (I took my tirade outside out of earshot of our toddler, because you know, therapy is expensive and I am trying not to fuck up my child.) He begged me like Hugh Grant in a cheesy rom-com. It wasn't attractive.

But in that moment I had a thought; one that could be the thing that started the healing; the thought of telling my daughter why Daddy wasn't there to tuck her in that night wasn't attractive either.

In fact, despite the hurt I was feeling at that moment, that seemed far more cruel and unusual.

Then the thought of myself; laying down in bed at night, hurt, and alone. That shit sucks too!

Why punish yourself some more? Yeah, I hated his guts and didn't want to see him. And I made him sleep on the couch... for a good, few nights. But at least he was *there.* He was there, and quite helpful with putting Em to bed. He was there in the morning to get me coffee and help start the day.

We were both hurting. But we were doing it together.

In full disclose, this stage was really awkward. Awkward silence. Awkward stares. Awkward conversation because he didn't know what to say to me and Lord knows I didn't have anything nice to say to him either.
I just don't want to give the misconception that having a cheating partner stay under the same roof is easy. It's certainly not. But I would argue that it's pro's outweigh the cons.

So, basically, my biggest and most important advice is the following:

Make the decision,
to **not make a decision.**

You have nothing to lose and everything to gain by simple pausing, and not making any decisions right away.

It's easy to say that strength is what allows us kick a cheating partner to the curb, but that's a bunch a bullshit. If we are honest with ourselves, it's ego and anger prompting that. Strength doesn't come from avoiding conflict, it comes from resolving it.

In this situation, it's easy to be mad. It's easy to want to punish. What isn't easy, is saying, "I just need a second here." The really fucking hard part is finding perspective before reacting. Showing restraint is strong. And really fucking hard.

But here's the most important thing to remember.

Your relationship is worth fighting for.
Until, of course, it isn't.

But you will never know, if you let your ego make the decisions, instead of your rational mind.

So, what if we can't get past this?
What if we do the work and realize that our relationship isn't worth saving?

First, that sucks. And if you haven't already heard it

from someone else, I'll be that friend that says, I'm sorry. I'm sorry you have to expierence this shit-storm.

But shit hasn't all gone to hell.
This wasn't all for nothing.

I'm going to go ahead and spell out what amazing qualities you'll have when you've done this kind of emotional work.

YOU WILL NOW HAVE

1. Peace of mind, just knowing you did your best to work it out will actually give you a decent bit of peace. You won't look back with doubts, wondering if you could've tried a little harder.
2. If you have kids, at the very least, they got X amount more months or years together as a family. When they are old enough, they will hopefully understand that you gave significant effort to forgive, and that your love of the family was what made you try to work it out. They will see that you believed in love and that it was worth fighting for. Despite no guarantees in life. That right there is an invaluable lesson and a way to bring something good out of something so, incredibly shitty.
3. You get to walk away with *less guilt*. (I can't say no guilt, because you will probably learn things about yourself through this process that are less than flattering, and you will understand your shortcomings in the relationship.) That may carry some guilt, but at least, once again, you *tried*. And you wouldn't believe me if I told you how consoling that is until you've felt it.

Here's the thing that is easy to lose sight of... just like the affair,

Some decisions just can't be taken back.

There *really* are very few re-do's in life, especially when it comes to the important stuff.

Right now, you are **mad**, and **hurt**, and **frustrated**;

Rightfully so.

So how the hell are you able to make such a monumental decision right now?

Strong, independent, intelligent women (and men!), get to be strong, independent, and intelligent by making rational, logical decisions.

What makes someone so successful, in let's say business, is their ability to look at a situation in its entirety and make a calculated decision based on facts.

If we consider our marriage to be the **most important contract we will ever enter**, how could we make a decision to alter or end it in the midst of an emotional crisis?

Simply, we can't.

Taking a pause is not *giving your partner a pass.*

It isn't saying that you are going to put up with this type of behavior. And it in no way guarantees that you will both live happily ever after... at least not necessarily *together.*

Feel free to show your significant other this section, if they seem to take your lack of immediate action as a sign of passiveness. It's not.

What does pausing *actually* mean?

Pausing means:

1. That you are an intelligent person, who very much values your relationship.
2. You are going to make a smart decision, based on logic and facts, not on ego and big feelings.
3. You are strong enough to do the hard work and you aren't afraid to get your hands dirty,
4. You are self-aware enough to know that you will be better prepared to make a decision, once the initial rush of emotions subsides.

We put so much thought into life's big decisions; buying a home or car, becoming a partner at work, our life insurance, but when it comes to ending a marriage, it is so often left to just our emotions.

Yes, obviously, you have to listen to your heart. But your heart *can* break, and it *can* heal again. That's why you have to listen to your head for a long while, and not just your broken heart.

**Your relationship is worth fighting for...
   until it isn't.**

Remember that? It bears repeating. (Something I will do a lot of in this, here, little book.)

> Not all cheaters are created equal.

IN THE TRENCHES

4 DIRTY TRUTHS

Know the details? Or play dumb?
This one is so, incredibly personal. (Like any of this isn't?)

I tell you what I chose, and the fallout from it, and then you can make your informed decision.

I *needed* to know the details.

Which unfortunately ended up coming out in long, drawn-out, dramatic revelations.

When I first confronted him about the email (which was a whole, hefty, 10 minutes after finding it), he only admitted to having a 'close friendship,' which *may* have crossed the lines of intimacy, but not in the physical/biblical sense.

He told me how they met at school and how she was struggling in the class. He was the honor student, so she initially asked him to tutor her. I mean, come on. This is the script to every bad romance novel. But he was away with the Coast Guard for 2 months at school. Away from his family. There was limited availability to even talk on the phone. In hindsight, I don't really know how much of his busyness was legitimate work or extracurricular. But he stuck to the just friends script; needless to say perhaps, but initially I knew he was lying.

But for the first couple days, he stuck to that version of the story.

The truth is, he isn't some sort of master manipulator that didn't want to get caught. (Although, let's keep it 100, and that was a little of the reason.) But the intense denial was rooted in trying to protect me. He really, really **didn't want to hurt me**. (Duh! He should've thought of that before he started the affair.)

That obvious fact aside, it was only now clear to him that if I knew what he had really done, that I would be crushed. He later admitted that he honestly never really gave a whole lot of thought about just how badly I would be hurt if I ever found out. He honestly thought at the time, that he could get away with it. But now, what was done, was done, and he thought that lying to me minimize the pain.

He wanted to spare me.

But the damage was done, and over the next few weeks, as each soul-crushing detail came to light, he finally realized that he was drawing out the hurt and that he needed to stop the bleed.
He needed to give me **all the facts**.

So, with his very hesitant blessing, I called her.

She answered. Then hung up.
So, I texted her... something to the effect of,
> 'I just want answers, and closure and at the very least, you f**king owe me this much.'

In just a few seconds, she called back.
And we talked.
For almost 2 hours.

Looking back on it, I can't believe she actually entertained the idea. I obviously needed it, but I think it probably helped her move on. She needed to realize how real I was. How real his and my life was.
I have gone back and forth on whether or not I want the details of what she said, and what their relationship consisted of to be public. Shoot, even as I write this, I'm still not convinced that I want this published. For so many reason, most importantly, for my children to potentially read one day.

As of now, neither our 5 nor 8-year-old know anything about what happened. I mean, why would they? They are obviously too young now, but I have really gone back and forth on whether I *ever* wanted them to know.

Specifically, our daughter. I have serious mixed feelings, *still,* on dimming the light that I think a little girl should have for her father.

But we are all human, and I feel like teaching her forgiveness might serve her better then continuing the idealistic-parent nonsense. I guess if you're reading this, then you know which path I chose.

But our conversation was a huge piece of the recovery puzzle for me, that needs not be left out.

*Let's just start off by saying that I was scary calm. I don't know if it was because I was 2 weeks away from my due date and all those hormones, but I just had a rush of calmness run over me. I calmly expressed my feelings...all those hopeless, tragic, you-just-destroyed-my-family feelings. She apologized, took responsibility and proceeded to answer my questions.

I'm just going to list a few of the details that she revealed to me...ones that were particularly poignant. And because, let's just be honest, *you want to know*.

- She had pursued him; and he was very honest about the fact that he was married, with a second baby on the way.

- He had no plans to leave me. But she was pushing him to continue some form of long distance relationship.

- They went on trips together, staying in hotels and sightseeing. (Which she posted to social media and I later found.) **Keep in mind, he was only an E-4, and money was seriously fucking tight.

- He met her family and was introduced as her boyfriend.

- She traveled back to our home together, slept in our bed, was there when the movers packed up our home, and he even introduced her to some of our friends that we had been stationed with. **This was a whammy. A serious, mind-fuck of a whammy.

What do you do with that kind of information?

Am I glad I had the opportunity to ask?
Yes, but that is some seriously complicated shit.

Like I mentioned before, I am the type of person who would have driven themselves crazy wondering and presumably, thinking the worst. The truth wasn't really any worse than I would have imagined it being.
So in that respect, I appreciated just *knowing.*
But damn if knowing all the dirty details isn't both a blessing and a curse.

On one hand, I believed her account of things. She didn't have anything to gain or lose in telling me the truth. My husband had a lot to gain by being dishonest, she did not. So, inherently, I believed her.

On the other hand, knowing the details of their relationship greatly increased the amount of 'triggers' that I would go on to expierence for years.

And those, my friends, are the nasty, little things that *really* do make forgiveness hard.

Triggers are places, songs, foods, cars, names, or just about anything that reminds you of the infidelity.

Just so happens I wrote a whole chapter on those little fuckers.

Knowing that they went to Philadelphia together and ate cheesesteaks made me want to fucking hate cheesesteaks. But honestly, who the fuck hates cheesesteaks? (Other than maybe, Vegans.)

I think you get the point, though...

Every time I ate a cheesesteak for the next 5 years, or anyone would mention Philly, I thought about her. I went so far as to sell our mattress because I found out she had slept on it once. I refused to ever sleep in it again. We slept for weeks in the spare bed in our sons room because we couldn't afford a new mattress yet.

My ego wouldn't afford me to sleep in the old one. I could've avoided all of that if I had just *not* asked for the details about their relationship.

On the other hand, I can't really say what it would be like if I hadn't found out. Would I have been able to find trust for him again without knowing he had put everything on the line? I mean, 'allowing' me to speak with her was a huge gesture of good faith on his part. So I question how we would have rebuilt, if I thought he was still somehow getting away with something by getting to keep the details hidden.

This may sound totally bat-shit to some, but some of the pain was appearing to come from being left out. The affair didn't include me, his partner. It was something that just the two of them shared. But we are in a partnership, and we shared everything. I wanted to somehow take that away from them. I wanted to take away the personal, intimate, private moments they shared. It was as if me being told about them, took away their value somehow.

Mind you, I wasn't thinking any of this in the moment. I was just thinking with my gut. I needed answers.

But when I really look back at *why* I probably needed those answers, it was less about needing to know, and more about control. In a twisted way, knowing was controlling. And that is one of those emotions that is really defeating after an affair; that feeling of loss of control. Especially for those of us that are strong, alpha-type personalities.

But, If I am being completely transparent, I wouldn't have made the same decision, if I had to do it over again.

I would still want to talk to her about a few things, most importantly, *did he have plans to leave me?*

But I wouldn't want to know all the details that I so intensely grilled her for. There were just some bits of information that probably did more harm than good in knowing.

I ended up following her on Facebook... bad idea!
She had posted so much about her 'boyfriend.'

Things that I wish I could un-see.

That created a whole heap of unnecessary hurt.
And I did that to myself.

Whether it's talking to the 'other person' or just talking to your partner about the details of their other relationships, make sure you know the ramifications of knowing the truth, before you start doing the asking.

It is totally okay to know about what generally happened without knowing the dirty details. "What you don't know wont hurt you" is painfully true.

Bottom line, do you think knowing the details will bring you closure, or do you think that the constant reminders would make forgiving too hard?

5 LOOSE LIPS

To tell, or not to tell? And *who* to tell?

When I first found out, I needed to tell *someone*. Typically, I would call my Mom or one of my closest girlfriends. But for some reason I hesitated. After exploring my feelings, I realized where my initial hesitation was stemming from.

Mom and Dad's marriage fell apart 18 years in, after an affair, so I knew that despite her best attempt, my Mom would have a difficult time giving me unbiased advice. I mean, how could it not biased? She's Mama Bear, and she's been in my shoes. Not only would her own decision possibly sway mine, but her hurt for me as well. I knew that she would be heart-broken that I was going through this, and I *knew* that would affect my decision making.

The similar thing can be said for any one of my amazing girlfriends. They have my back, fiercely, and would probably have shouted for me to 'leave his ass!' Not to say my girlfriends don't support my marriage, because they absolutely do. But as strong women, we tend to be very protective of each other. Especially when it comes to men. They too, were biased.

But I needed to talk to someone.
And I bet you do, too.

So, who do you reach out to?
The best answer:

Someone who loves you, and your partner collectively.
And ones whose initial reaction would be to work things out.

That may be a therapist. It may be a friend of the family. It may be a Pastor or religious leader.

For me, it was my Step-Mother-in-law. (Yes, you read that right. My husband's, Dad's, second wife.) Not at all a strange choice. Am I right? Ok, perhaps not the most obvious person to reach out to, but this was actually one of my better life decisions. Here's why:

1. She isn't his Mom, so she isn't on the my-son-is-perfect train. The last thing I needed was even a inkling of someone taking his side. Although it's imperative to mention, that when I did tell his Mom, she was amazingly supportive. (Even though up until that point, she did partly believe that her son could do no wrong.) But her support of us was such a huge blessing, and something that ended up bringing us so much closer as women.
2. She's a woman with more life expierence, and years of marriage under her belt then my peers had.
3. She loves him and would be able to remind me of the good in him. (Even if I didn't always want to hear it.)
4. Most importantly, I knew she wanted us to survive as a couple, and family unit.

I fully realize that not everyone has a close relationship with their partners' family. Honestly, I didn't realize that I had that kind of relationship with them until shit hit the fan.

But I would encourage talking to someone who really does have both of your best interests at heart.

Going through infidelity in a marriage often leaves us feeling totally isolated. Those feelings of failure and shame that almost always accompany the infidelity are dark and somewhat embarrassing and that can make it difficult to open up.

When someone gets cancer, there is no shame or embarrassment, or failure associated with a medical diagnosis, so you tell your community, and thus, you receive support; support crucial to getting better. But that isn't the case after an affair. It's still seen as shameful to society. Speaking of medical diagnosis, in conversations when I have opened up about what my husband and I went through, I often associate infidelity with mental illness. Both something out of the 'victims' control, both emotionally crippling, both needing support to recover, both still attached to stigmas of shame and failure.

Let me make this abundantly clear, finding someone to confide in is crucial.

I, myself, don't really care for 'bothering people with my problems.' (Which admittingly is probably contributing to the whole stigma of asking for help is somehow weak... but that's where I was, or am.) So, reaching out to people outside my usual circle was super uncomfortable for me at first.

Like *really* uncomfortable.

I want you to stop feeling; take emotion out of the equation completely and **look again at this one logically**.

You need a sounding board.
Two heads are better than one, right?
One might argue that the best ideas come from a group of intelligent people giving their input on one topic.

You can also approach going to a therapist or counselor in this way... That is, if you have some aversion to it. You seek the advice of an doctor when you get a cold. But if your cold doesn't go away, you may seek a second opinion. With a legal issue, you will probably consult a lawyer. You may also run it by your cousin's fiancé who just passed the bar exam at Sunday dinner. If you are trying to lose weight, you may try a diet, and you may also ask a couple of your friends who saw results for some pointers. All of these re the same scenario, different application. When we have problems, it's our nature to reach out for help. So don't let the topic change your normal behavior.

WHEN AND HOW TO TELL YOUR INNER CIRCLE:

There really is no magic answer for this one.

My best suggestion is to tell your closest friends once you have sorted through all your feelings enough to know what directions/actions you are going to take... or at least which direction you are leaning.

I like the *'this is how I'm doing, how I'm going to move forward, and _____ is how you could support me'* approach.

It will eliminate the opportunity for haters, because you've already made up your mind. (Using that phrase lightly, because you will most likely go back and forth as you work through everything.) **But it will give your friends ideas on <u>how</u> to be supportive.**

When it comes to families, some are understanding, some like to hold grudges. In any case, most parents will look at their kids significant other differently once they know they have hurt them. As parents, our job is to protect our kids, and it's hard for some people to forgive those that have hurt their children.

If this sounds like your Mom, Dad, brothers or sisters, you *may* want to keep this inside the marriage. It really isn't anyone's business.

No one has *the right to know*.
It is totally acceptable to keep things private.

*Side note: That doesn't mean you need to lie or cover-up for the cheater. But deliberately choosing to keep negative energy and thoughts out of the relationship is a mature, logical decision for any relationship.

Again, if you *do* choose to tell your family, I would again approach it similarly to what I suggested for your close friends.

Tell them whatever <u>facts you feel like sharing</u>, <u>what decisions you've made</u> to get past it, and <u>how they can be supportive moving forward</u>.

Personally, I didn't tell my Mom for almost two years for a mix of reasons. I think you will probably relate to these.

I didn't want to admit failure.

Which, of course, is absurd. Right?

*Being lied to, cheated on, or going through a difficult time in your relationship is **not a failure**.*

But it's easy to see it as one.
Especially when you are in the trenches.

Admitting to my Mom that my picture-perfect marriage, wasn't so picture perfect was something that I had to work up to. And while she did take the news in stride, and with class, in full disclosure, she was a little upset I didn't tell her sooner.

She was hurt that I didn't want to confide in her. And I totally understand that. And I was prepared for it.

But she also respected my decision. And my desire to work on my marriage instead of just quitting when the going gets tough.

She also shared a tid-bit with me that shed some light on her marriage to my Dad. She told me that while she is happier in her relationship now, and although she didn't really have the choice when it came to the ending of their marriage, she did say that she wished things could've been different with Dad.

Without devaluing the relationship she has with my now-Stepfather, I think that was her way of saying, she wished she had been able to do something to save her marriage.

But like I've said before, we don't all get that choice.

In the end, having people to confide in is crucial when going through something traumatic. Whatever it is.

Even more so when going through something traumatic, that still has a stigma attached to it. And let's be honest;

> Staying with a 'cheater' still has a stigma attached to it.

On the days when it gets hard, and forgiveness seems impossible, having a friend remind you of *how in love you used to be*, can be the one thing that gets you through another day.

So, whoever it is, be it a neighbor, or a random Mom at school, be vulnerable, open up and **tell someone**.

6 HOT TOPICS

1. Jealousy

Some of us are jealous by nature, some not so much.

But after being cheated on, there are few that walk away without it. The trick is being able to sort out the difference between true warning signs, and the fantasies that are so easy to believe.

If you do a Renegotiation Contract, like I suggest in **CHAPTER 9**, then your partner will probably be on a proverbial leash for some time. And honestly, that time will help tremendously with the jealousy issue, if for no other reason than it will cut down on the opportunities to be jealous.

If (s)he isn't going to the bar after work with friends, there is no opportunity to be jealous or nervous about who they are with, or what they might do.

It *really* lessens the trauma and fear of it happening again and the constant worry of having to relive that. Because that's what it all comes down to, right?

> If they did this once, could they do it again?

And the answer to that is one crazy, messed up reality, but it's also, very simple.

> There is really no certainty in life.
> There is no black and white.

It's learning to find happiness in the grey area.

Worrying that something bad is going to happen to you, isn't going to somehow lessen your changes of it happening. Worrying *will*, however, make you crazy.

After a while, you'll gradually get used to your new, grey, normal. And while that sounds super depressing, it's actually a really good thing. It means you have found your stride.

So, what then?
What happens when they *do* want to go on that guys trip?

Even after they have earned back your trust? You could easily slip into thoughts of temptation and opportunity. And you wouldn't be *totally* wrong.

2. Wedding Rings
This is a controversial topic in the traditional therapy world. Most therapists would agree, that it is best for a marriage if both partners continue to wear their rings. (Assuming you already did. But this type of display of commitment can come in other forms such as other jewelry, but also in things such as tattoos. To which, these feelings still apply.)

Personally, as soon as I found out about the affair, I wanted to take them off and chuck them at his face. (I'm pretty sure I did do that at some point in the aftermath.)

And for what I learned in my research, that is a **super common** feeling. They *were* a symbol of your commitment to each other.

Commitment broken, rings off.

While it would be hard for anyone to argue that feeling this way isn't justified, it also doesn't really help anything. And truthfully, it may feel good. At least for a few minutes, then it's going to feel terrible. I promise you. I know, that is giving it to you straight, with little sugar coating. It *will* feel like shit. At some point. If you go from wearing your wedding rings every day, to taking them off in anger. You will, almost certainly, regret that decision at some point, and will want to put them back on.

With that said, I am not necessarily advocating you continue to wear them either.
I'll argue both sides:

1. They can become a trigger. If you've been married for a while, you probably hardly notice your rings. They are just there. But after an affair, you may start to notice them more. And it can uncomfortable. Like, 'what do these even symbolize anymore?' Your once favorite piece of jewelry could now become your daily reminder of hurt and pain.
2. If you are fortunate enough to have a pricy rock, it can feel like a sham. "Here's this big diamond to cover up my

sham of a marriage." (Ok, that was a little dramatic, but you probably understand what I mean.) Even a more modest wedding set (like mine), seemed like I was showing off a perfect marriage, which couldn't have been further from the truth.

> **I shouldn't have to put this disclaimer, but I will….
> Wearing a wedding ring, no matter the monetary value, is not inherently shoving your perfect marriage in anyone's face. You simply wearing your ring doesn't mean your unmarried best friend feels like you are rubbing it in. But after an affair, or any type of loss of trust, you can easily start to over-analyze the meaning behind everything. And when you start to question everything… even the smallest details can be consuming.

But please don't let this dictate your feelings. If you still love wearing your wedding rings, **wear them proudly!**

I did stop wearing mine for a while. If I didn't say that, it would be unfair to you. But since hindsight is 20/20, here are a few, better, suggestions.

1. Wear just your wedding band. It's probably smaller, and more discreet. It will symbolize that you are still married and working on it, but it also gives you some control and boundaries. You won't flash the rock that he gave you. (Since most men see it as a status-level statement too.) Call it a power move if you want to, but shit does it feel good to take some power back after being drug through this mess.
2. If you have something that fits, wear another ring on that finger. Maybe one from a parent, grandparent, friend or even one your bought yourself. I started wearing ring that my grandmother gave me. She was such a strong woman,

and such an inspiration to me. I felt like I still wanted to 'look married' to the world, and this was a good way to accomplish that and give me strength.

3. Allow your partner to buy you another one. It shouldn't be expensive. This isn't an 'I'm sorry' gift, that's lavishness trumps its thoughtfulness. Although a few years 'late,' my husband eventually gifted me a simple silver band, inscribed with "I will love you forever." That would've been awesome in those first few months. Also, this is what I call an opportunity to succeed. (Feel free to jump to that chapter to hear more about that awesomeness.)

Choosing one of these suggestions, or just continuing to wear your original wedding rings, will be a huge sign of hope for your partner.

It's a sign that you are willing to see this through this and find a way to forgive and more forward.

In the same respect, taking them off completely, sends the message that you're done.

And maybe you feel like you are.

But if you're reading this, then I know deep down, you aren't done.

Why make the process harder by taking away your partners hope?
That just isn't helpful.

---

3. Explaining the 'Why?'

Why did he cheat?
Why did he lie?
What could I have done better?
What could I have done to make him fulfilled with me?

There is a lot to this.
Let's just start by stating the (hopefully) obvious:

> There is nothing that you could have done to make your partner not cheat.

It's that simple. And that complicated.

Knowing why is not going to make it hurt less.
Or prevent it from happening again.

If someone is feeling drawn to cheating, they are, or are not going to go through with it, based on their feelings and moral compass. At the end of the day, it is a very selfish, and lonely decision. And once this is on persons radar, there is very little that you can do to change that.

With that said, there are many, small decisions that lead up to an affair. (Again, typically speaking. I am not talking about the random alcohol-induced hook-up; though, even then, it still applies a little too. No one has every blamed good decisions on alcohol.)

It's the attention from the secretary after you guys have had a fight over miscommunication. It's the server at the restaurant he frequents that's consoling him after overhearing him vent to his co-workers how you were on him about something involving his job, etc.

Those scenarios breed most affairs; opportunistic little

fucks. But where does that leave couples? We cant have a disagreement without worry that it could be the small domino that gets the line tumbling? Of course not. Almost every couple is going to have disagreements.

This is the cold, hard truth; there is no reason to mess up a healthy, strong, loving relationship.

Meaning, if you are looking for 'why,' you may not like the answer. (Don't hate me for saying that!)

Because there is **no good answer to that question.**

Now, the brutally honest part. (That applies to probably 99% of us.)

You *do* share 'blame' in the relationship not being as strong as it could be, or as open as it could be.

That is just common sense. You don't have to be entirely self-aware to know that you aren't perfect.

But in some relationships, it is easy to reflect and see what you could've done better. You may know already, that you were equally guilty for the less-than-stellar state of your relationship before the affair.

In other relationships, you may actually be somewhat innocent in regards to 'blame.' Some people are actually quite good in relationships; in being open, and generous, and loving.

That nasty truth still remains; in either situation, **you couldn't have prevented the affair from happening.**

Acceptance of this fact is the first step to gaining back control.

**Because when you release blame,
you gain control, by choosing to let it go.**

---

4. Snooping
Yep. All of us have either done it, or thought about it.

Regardless of if you have ever found something or not, this is a tricky practice.
It's also a very attractive one after mistrust.
And let's be real, this isn't a new practice. Women have been smelling their man's collar for millennia.
 (Yes, that sounds incredibly sexist, however true.)

Now, in addition to the laundry sniffing and wallet checking, we have credit card monitoring, email checking, text, DM, Facebook… the list goes on and on.

Checking the phone! Right?
 Why do you even have a password, anyway?

While you may drive yourself crazy wondering what they might be doing behind your back, you may really also be driving yourself crazy thinking there *is* something going on behind your back.

And, again, finding something isn't going to actually help anything.

If your partner stayed after you found out about the affair, then they passed on their opportunity to be with someone else. They are choosing to make the effort to fix your relationship. They chose to end the affair.

Stop looking for ways to sabotage it.

If you really think they're still cheating, even with

everything that you are going through, then you just need to be honest with them and breakdown exactly what they are doing that is making you feel that way.

On the other hand, if they did it once, they *could* do it again, so ultimately, you have to do what you have to do . But be prepared for things getting dirty.
If your partner is being faithful, this is going to come as a real blow to them and your progress. All for what?

Once again, if they are still cheating, you will eventually find something. Without having to look too closely. If you are doing the steps, and having honest communication, and they are *still* messing around, you will know. Because now, if you weren't already, you are tuned in.

I'm not saying to just trust blindly, because obviously it's not crazy to believe that if someone did something like this once, they are capable to do it again. But you *do* have to believe that if they are going through the steps to work things out, you have to believe that they are acting in a way that honors the relationship. And if they aren't, it isn't going to take crazy snooping to find it. It will, at some point, reveal itself.

7 TRIGGERS

Like I mentioned in Chapter 3, I needed to put a name to the circumstances that began to haunt me. Turns out, there is one, and it's a pretty common term. But come 2009, it wasn't in my vocabulary.

<u>Triggers</u> are things that reminds you of the infidelity.

They can be places, songs, food, cars, names, or just about anything you can imagine.

Keeping it 100%?

They are *often* unavoidable.

In my case...
We went on an overnight date to a Zac Brown Band concert in Atlanta to try and rekindle things. Since we had young children, I usually used a diaper bag as a purse. We had some time to kill, so my husband mentioned that it was almost Mother's Day and he wanted to pick me out a new purse. One that didn't need to be big enough to fit diapers in it. Pretty solid gesture. So we went to check out the Atlanta mall. We found a purse that we both loved. Then we glanced at the tag...

The designers' name is the same as 'hers'. Well isn't that just an awesome fucking coincidence?

And there, in a one-second-glance, the tone of the date and the vibe between us, melted.

This will happen.
Often.

It's that constant reminder, even after you have worked through a lot of the grief, and have consciously decided to forgive, that makes moving forward so difficult.

But they are also <u>opportunities</u>.

Most traditional therapists will advise, the way for a relationship to survive infidelity, is to not talk about it once you have discussed everything there is to be discussed. That for forgiveness to happen, the affair shouldn't be dangled over your partners head for the eternity of the relationship.

That is valid. As it really isn't fair, in any capacity, to constantly be reminded of our failures.

And here we are again, at one of those grey area situations.

After the first few months, I started to feel like I should keep my feelings to myself if I was triggered by something when we were having a good time.

I didn't want it to be *my fault* that the energy shifted.

I didn't want *any* of the situation to feel like my fault.

After some weeks of attempting to hold in my feelings, my husband finally brought it up in therapy. He mentioned how I still seemed like I was struggling sometimes, but I wasn't opening up about it.

In my case, my husband is generally pretty observant, and he is definitely tuned into my feelings and mood. So for him, it was obvious. If you have a partner that is slightly more oblivious, it may be a little less noticeable. But it doesn't take an emotional genius to notice when you are having a good time with someone and all of a sudden their mood changes.

My husband told our therapist how he wished that I would open up in the moment and tell him what triggered me. I still have to laugh at the idea that he actually wanted me to tell him more of how much of fucked up situation this is. But it makes sense, ain't shit more awkward than not acknowledging the drunk, naked elephant in the room.

But through trial and error, we discovered something:
<u>**Being honest was a way for him to console me.**</u>

In my mind, bringing it up would only upset him, and possibly start an argument. Instead, we realized that ignoring the triggered feelings, is really a missed opportunity to <u>show support and earn trust</u>.

Back at that department store:
He could probably read it all over my face when I saw

the label. But when I showed him, he grabbed my hand, looked into my eyes and mouthed, "I love you. I'm sorry." And without a beat, then added for a tad of humor, "it's not even that cute, I know we can find you something better." He may have added a little, "fuck that bitch, anyway." Or was that me?

And right then, we were back on track. Crazy, right?
I could have stewed on it and let it upset me.

I didn't even attempt to hide my feelings.

And here is the mind-blowing part; **my feelings were met with love, empathy and understanding.**

Which is in little supply after an affair, so I was going to take all of it that I could get.
It turned into a moment that made us closer, because he immediately gained back trust. The way he reacted earned him trust. The way he put *his* feelings aside, and thought about what I was feeling.

I immediately started believing again that he was my partner and <u>was there for me emotionally</u>.

> Turns out, honestly *really is* the best policy.

But what if my partner responds with anger?

I gave full disclosure in the beginning of this book, that not every relationship is worth saving.

How your partner deals with your emotions, is arguably **the most critical part of moving forward.**

If I had been honest with my husband and he reacted

with frustration, anger, attitude, or defensiveness, that would have given me some insight that our relationship probably wasn't going to recover. And that maybe it wasn't even worth it.

You are not just healing from an 'affair.'

You are trying to recover from the emotional destruction that comes more from being let down by the person in life that is supposed to be your primary emotional supporter.

Your partner has just let you down in such a monumental fashion, that the full acceptance of wrongdoing is absolutely critical for moving forward.

And doing so with humility, kindness and not a hint of ego.

You deserve that.

If you can't trust your partner enough to open up about your triggers…or if when you do, they respond with anger… You may be in a cut-your-losses situation. Because the truth is, this is an upfill battle, and it requires a lot of humility on your partner's part. Sure, it's easy to get defensive when something we have done wrong is continually a topic of conversation. But your partner, should at some point, be able to remove themselves from some situations and realize, it's no longer just about what they *did,* but rather, what they *can do* now.

8 SETTLING THE SCORE

Revenge sex, hall-pass, opportunistic fuck… so many variations for a very similar thought process.

And just so happens, it's the one topic that no one wants to talk about. Openly.

But I am going to go ahead and say it out loud.

Everyone who gets cheated on, in the depths of their pain, will consider some version of revenge sex.

I went ahead and said everyone, because from what I could find, just about everyone has this thought cross their mind, in some capacity. It might just be flirting in front of them to make them jealous. Or it may go way beyond the somewhat innocent nature of that thought.

You will, at some point, feel like you want to hurt the person who hurt you, by somehow retaliating.

It's not just the crazy ones.
Sorry, not sorry.

Eye for an eye is how old? It's human nature.

The real difference here, is obviously, whether or not you go through with it. But just the thought, it totally, completely, normal.

I will go ahead and tell you my decision up front, so you know my bias from the start.

I chose to keep committed to my vows.

Before I sound all higher-than-thou, let me make it clear; I had a few *cough cough* partners before my husband, so I didn't feel like I was 'missing out' on the opportunity to have something that I had missed out on by being married. I was also literally two weeks from my due date when I found out about the affair, so in the aftermath, I was fully immersed in the newborn stage of childrearing. Not to mention our toddler, new city, husband's new job and the renovations of our 100 year old home.

I was busy, and tired, and not really feeling any sort of sexual healing. I didn't need it physically. Emotionally, I was full; overflowingly full.

I had plenty of things going on in my head, trying to go and add something to the mix didn't sound appealing to me in the least.

But this won't be, and often isn't, everyone's reaction.

Some of you might find out in your sexual peak. Some of you may wish you could have some sexy time with a coworker, shit maybe even a stranger! And if those are anything like what you're feeling, there aren't a lot of resources that talk about the gnarly feelings your likely to encounter. So, here is my list of some of those thoughts that may creep in, and what to do when they do.

REVENGE SEX

I don't think thats is a traditionally defined term yet, but I would define it as *having a sexual encounter with someone, other than your partner, in the act of revenge. Often, although not always intentionally to hurt the feelings of, or to make your partner jealous.*

i.e. You find out your partner cheated. A couple weeks later, when you are out with your friends, you go home with someone you meet on the dance floor.
Because, hey, they did it too... right?

Or you intentionally hit on the server at the restaurant to make your partner jealous. Or you start hanging out with that one friend at work that your partner was already a little skeptical about.

If you are feeling this way, I hear you. But if you haven't yet acted on it, here are some logical things to consider before you do.

If you do go ahead and pursue someone, out of revenge, <u>you will almost certainly regret it</u>.

Maybe not right away.
But in most people, the guilt *will* set in.

This should not be confused with the crazy, slight chance that you meet your soul mate and you choose to act opportunistically.

If that's the case... then you, do you.

For everyone else, expect to add guilt and shame to your already emotionally-fragile self.

If for no other reason...

I suggest you **hold-off, in the interest of self-love**.

There are actually a long list of reasons to hold-off.

Breaking the promise of monogamy to your partner is a big deal. You have a painful understanding of that right now. So again, how are *you* supposed to make a life-altering decision when you are in this emotional state?

It goes back to why I say that we can't make a decision to leave a long-term, committed relationship, when we are in the midst of the emotional roller-coaster.

You just can't. You aren't thinking clearly.

Now more than ever, you need to be self-aware enough to know that you can't make a good, rational, un-biased decision that will effect the rest of your life right now.

And that's okay.
That's the secret.

> You don't have to decide anything right now.

Did you get that?
Or maybe you should read that again?

HALL PASS

You may, or may not, be hip to the meaning of this term. But it usually refers to a celebrity, and in the rare case *that someone might meet their celebrity crush, they have the permission of the partner to pursue said celebrity in whatever manner seems appropriate.*

i.e. Make out backstage, roadie on the tour bus, run into the drummer in the lobby of your hotel... you get the idea, right?

Thing is, most people don't just randomly run into their celebrity crush at the bar, hit it off, and have the opportunity for it to go any farther.

So, why the heck am I even mentioning it?

A couple years into the recovery process, I found myself feeling stagnant with our intimacy. We had dealt with most everything by now, and we were back to being intimate. (Although, not quite to where we were before.)

I started to develop feelings of jealousy that he got to live out this sort of fantasy, and I was still 'stuck' with just him forever.

Nasty thought?
I told you this gets dirty.

We've all heard about the fear of missing out.

When I finally sorted through these feelings, and had the guts to speak openly about them to my husband, I quickly realized the shift.

You have the upper hand.

Depending on your level of ethics when it comes to blackmailing your partner; you are in an interesting position to look at this as the fucked up part of the negotiation.

Maybe you are a very sexual person, and monogamy isn't something that comes completely naturally.
But you've been committed.

You *may* see this as an opportunity to negotiate your hall-pass. Or even less fucked up sounding, maybe this is the time to re-negotiate the terms of your relationship when it comes to monogamy. Maybe it isn't working for either of you.

One scenario that you might consider is one that allows, should you find yourself in the position that you are attracted to someone, and there is the opportunity for it to be intimate, that you have permission to act on it.

Is that crazy? Maybe.
Is that my suggestion? Not necessarily.

But that's the beauty of relationships.
Everyone's is different.

I'm not a prude, and I believe that any relationship is valid, as long as there is open communication and everyone is on the same page.
What it really comes down to is simple.

After an affair, there is a major shift in power.

One person holds all the cards, and one is trying to win them back. And by cards, I mean <u>love and affection</u>.

There is no longer an even balance of power.

That upper hand can really show up especially loud when it comes to taking 'blame' in arguments. And this sensitive topic will very quickly escalate to an argument if you aren't prepared.

I strongly suggest that if you are experiencing any thoughts of being unfaithful, that you bring this topic up in therapy. (Or to whoever you are opening up to.)

Even if you don't hear what you want to hear.

Traditional therapists probably aren't going give you the green light to go and have intimacy with someone other than your partner.

Two 'wrongs' don't make a right... right?

I use the word wrongs cautiously. If you are given permission, then technically it isn't wrong in the traditional sense of the word. But if you have a monogamous relationship, then in whatever the scenario, being not-monogamous would be breaking the boundaries of the relationship. And if you believe in monogamy from a fundamental standpoint, you will almost certainly have ill feeling in the end.
But ultimately, these feelings of wanting some extra spice will probably linger for a while, so it will serve you to communicate it with your partner.

Personally, I did expierence this is some capacity. I knew that I didn't want anything to do with the revenge aspect of being with someone else. But I *was* jealous that he got to have another first kiss. That he got to expierence those butterflies that happen when you meet someone. He got to expierence all those fun, exciting things that I was left out of.

I was jealous.
Jealous that he got to have that kind of excitement.
Jealous that I didn't.

I felt like if I was staying, doing my work to forgive, and move forward; then my reward was that if I ever found myself really attracted to someone, that I would be able to pursue it.

At the time, that seemed fair.

And despite all common sense, he very reluctantly, 'agreed' to my hall-pass.

I put the quotes because he really didn't want to.
But he had to.

Because I had all the power.
    <u>I</u> held the power.

He probably thought that I would leave him if he said no.
I probably did nothing to dispel that.

Round-about blackmail?
    Again, I told you this would get dirty.
There is a reason why there is such an issue with the abusive of power.

Truth is, after 5 years, I would be lying if I said that

when we have gone through something tough, and are fighting more than usual, the thought still occasionally crosses my mind. (We will touch on that in a bit.)

But I have never even gotten remotely close to, or even seriously entertained, the idea in a specific situation.

But the decision to follow through is going to come with consequences. Serious ones.

Sure, you will have settled the score. And maybe you got to have those firsts again. However, you *must be clear* that your decision could be what finalizes the end of your relationship.

Just because you chose forgiveness and to stay in the relationship, doesn't mean that they are going to return in kind.

That sound pretty messed up? Do I dare tell you that after you stayed after the affair and tried to work things out, that your partner may not be up for the same fight? I'd be an ass if I didn't at least warn you. They may be emotionally spent. They might not be up for the fight.

The question you'll really need to ask yourself is this: And after being a victim of infidelity, do you really want to feel like it was *your choices* that ended the relationship?

There comes that damn guilt and shame again.

THE TAKEAWAY

Even if you *just talk about* the hall-pass, you have to understand the consequences.

My husband is reluctant every time I go out with my girlfriends. He doesn't say much, but I know he feels insecure about it.

Is that because I said that I *might,* in the future, pursue my own interests?

You bet it is.
I can't say that I regret communicating my feelings.

I really needed full honesty at that point.

But I also understand, that with that honesty, came the weight of knowing that I was causing him pain too.

In hindsight, and knowing how much he has done to get this relationship back on track, that is a heavy burden to bear. A weight that despite his best efforts to get past, still creeps up. A weight that I would take off his shoulders if I could.

This is *that* topic that I seriously suggest you give extra thought and time to before acting on. I am usually for full-disclosure on blatant honestly, but you really can't take something back once it's been said.

Again, just pause and then reassess.

MOVING FORWARD

9 RENEGOTIATION CONTRACT

This is one of those practical exercises that you can actually *do* right now to help get your relationship back on track.
This step is an absolute must.

I don't know how we would have navigated those crucial month's/years without this.

So, what exactly is a renegotiation contract?

Usually, in the beginning stages of any relationship, there are certain boundaries and expectations that are generally agreed upon. They range from how we behave, carry ourselves, to who and how we interact with people outside the relationship. Typically this comes gradually and naturally, as situations occur over the course of the relationship.

For example, dating when you're a young adult:
Mark is turning 21. Sophie still 19. Mark wants to go out to a bar to celebrate his birthday with friends, but Sophie is underage. The conversation that follows is a negotiation; who is comfortable with what, in that specific scenario. Maybe Sophie isn't comfortable with Mark going out to the bar without her

because drinking can lead to questionable decisions. Mark disagrees. And so on…

In a healthy relationship, this is where the balanced, natural negotiation would come in. Maybe Mark offers to check in, or offers to have a certain, trouble-making friend not attend. Sophie might add in a suggestion, for a quick video chat. What each couple decides is right for them isn't the point.

The negotiation is the point.

And it is something that we really ought to be taught.

It is something that continues throughout life in general, but especially in intimate relationships.

So, here is the 're' in the renegotiation.

Let's use Mark and Sophie again.
Fast forward 10 years, they are married with two kids. After years of earning trust, Sophie had relaxed her ideas on Mark going out with friends, and they had enjoyed years of respectful outings without each other. Until Mark had an affair. Cue the renegotiation.

Redefining what is, or is not acceptable in specific situations is a huge game changer.

Make it a contract.
Just like a marriage contract, lease or mortgage.

Write it down. Shoot, sign it!
Make it, and both of your feelings, legitimate.
And take this opportunity to make all your expectations known.

I should note, this is the time to get out ALL the feelings and issues in the relationship, not just those pertaining to the affair.

So, want to know what was actually in ours?

(We actually didn't take my above advice, and didn't write it down, but we *did* take notes and talk about it in therapy, so we had a third party to hold us accountable...)

But here is the gist of it:

1. No dinner & drinks with friends or co-workers without the spouses or families. This was a big one for us, since my husband's affair started after an evening at Applebee's with co-workers. Yep. Cue eye roll and warranted judgements. But there was *no* feasible way for me to totally move forward if he continued the behavior that lead to the affair.

2. No alone time with someone of the opposite sex. Ever. **This one was hard. (Especially since he was Active Duty Military.) But this was important to me since in my situation, he was almost duped into the affair. She had her sights set on him when she asked him to 'tutor her' and they hung out a lot before they crossed lines. So, I didn't just *want* this, I *needed it*. I needed to know that he wouldn't put himself in ANY position, innocent or not, that could *lead to something*.

So, no shared car rides, no alone time in the office, no 'partner' workouts. And believe me, we went into detail. If he was alone in the office and a female walked in, he was to make sure that both doors were open, and if possible, he was to find a reason to walk outside or down the hall.
Think this sounds trivial? Totally overbearing?
I get it. I do.
But I think this was the most crucial parts of moving forward for a few reasons.

The first, by him <u>just agreeing to new terms showed me that he was willing to do the things necessary to earn back trust.</u> Even if it meant having to go out of his way, or having an uncomfortable conversation. He also earned back trust, little by little, when he would mention that he had to step outside when Ms. Whoever walked in. And finally, the obvious one; once I started to actually trust that he was following through with our conditions, I knew that he was being respectful to me, and aware of possibly compromising positions.

<u>3. No Instagram B**ches / Cleaning up social media.</u> Now, I have always been pretty comfortable in my skin, so I never really thought twice about my husband acknowledging someone else's beauty. Yep. That s**t changed.

Not only was I post-partum, but after the affair, his open admiration of others now seemed far less innocent. So even though social media played no role in his affair, this was still a necessary change to our original partnership.

I will also note that there are certain circumstances where your partner might require a social media presence for his career. However, if your partner's online persona is continually causing an issue in the relationship, you may be at an impasse. Either ya'll discuss it, and some boundaries are set, or they go into a new line of work.

It's that simple. And that complicated.

While many professions pose an arguable need for a social media presence, it could still be used as an opportunity to be unfaithful.

A lot of this is common sense. It's just not talked about... until it becomes a problem. So whatever your particular issues with social media may be, I suggest you take the time to get them **all** out now. Lay some ground rules and set some tangible expectations that you can both adhere to.

4. More Social Media Rules: post about your relationship.

Again, this will be slightly different for everyone. For us, my husband said his Insta account was only to share about his life. If that's the case, give a shout-out to your awesome kids or wife now and then. (Instead of only posting about your fishing adventures.)

This is a good time to mention that if you haven't read up on how we are different in the way we give and receive love, you need to. Some of us need affection, some need praise, some need it publicly, some privately. Do your research and outline clearly and boldly to each other what makes you tick.

For me, when he publicly declared his love for everything else, but not for the family that he supposedly 'adores,' that felt like a dis to me. Again, before you judge, this actually gave him the opportunity to succeed.

Trying to earn someone's trust after you've lost it seems like the impossible mountain to climb. This was an easy way for him to win brownie points. A simple, tangible way he could make me feel loved and appreciated. This is something that he continues to do... he knows it's a simple gesture to make me smile.

5. Go to therapy.

I am a firm believer in therapy. Whether it be spiritually based, or traditional psychology; having a non-biased person to talk to is irreplaceable. **Unfortunately, in this world, not everyone has access to traditional therapy. I know I talked about this in Chapter 5, but if that's your situation, I strongly urge you to find local, non-profit options. Local religious organizations usually have someone, and often you can find local options in the community.
Even if you go once. Even if you only go to someone and have them help you with the renegotiating.

I requested that my husband go alone; to deal with, or open up about things that he didn't want to say in front of me.
He requested that we go to some together.

We did both.

(Just so happens, that our therapist that we went to together was the first person to introduce me to the idea of the renegotiation contract in the first place!)

<u>6. A Vow Renewal.</u> If down the road, we found that we were able to navigate this major shit-storm in our relationship, and I had found a way to not only forgive, but to actually let go of the hurt and move on; then I needed him to retake our vows.

In my mind, he broke the first promise, and just saying he wouldn't do it again, didn't seem like enough.

I had given up a business I loved, I was following him and his military career around the country, and I was being the literal example of a supportive wife. (No, I wasn't perfect, but I had put the family, and him first and had asked for little in return.)

I needed a gesture. A big one.

I needed to believe that he really was in this for the long haul. I needed to feel like the decisions I made for our family weren't in vain. I needed to feel that deep connection and love toward him, that had been long gone since the news dropped.

We needed a do-over.
So, we created one.
For our 5-year anniversary, about two years after the affair, we renewed our vows, surrounded by family, on a beach in Oahu.

While all of these steps, and requests could easily be laughed off as unnecessary and I'm sure some people will do just that. But I promise you, that if nothing else, this process of forgiveness will reveal how important acknowledgement of your feelings and expectations are in a relationship.

You have everything to gain... or lose. Depending on how you look at it. This is the time to put all your cards on the table and tell your partner what *you* need to feel loved and secure. Talk about it. Negotiate. Listen to your partner's feelings as well. * That is important to note; this isn't supposed to be a one-way conversation.

The Renegotiation Contract should apply to both partners. Now, you may choose to make two different ones, and might agree that you have different needs and requests. That is okay too. A long as this isn't a list of demands that you create, and they must follow. Instead, this is the most important mediation you've ever been a part of.
No pressure.

> Good people can do bad things.
> And still be good people, deserving of love.

10 OPPORTUNITIES TO SUCCEED

I was your typical teenager, when it came to pushing boundaries. I never really went too far, but I was born with in innate sense of 'why' and I was very skeptical of just doing things because I was told to. I wasn't a rebel without a cause; in fact I had many of them. But I still questioned, and pushed back in a way that was still, more or less, playing by everyone's rules. Nonetheless, instead of getting a car for my sixteenth birthday, like almost everyone else at school, Mom told me I didn't deserve one yet. I needed to earn it; meaning my behavior had to prove to her that I was responsible enough that responsibility. (Keep in mind that I grew up in a very affluent town. While my family didn't have the amount of wealth that other students had, we still were plenty comfortable. It sounds snotty, but everyone *was* getting a car for their birthday. It didn't just *seem* like that. Time and place, I suppose.) While the situation may differ, most of us can relate with a parent (or a teacher or coach), asking us to work for something without telling us *how*.

How, exactly, is someone supposed to prove they have earned something?
That's the million-dollar question.

My Mom (though generally a really, good parent) didn't have a *specific* answer.

I already got good grades. (Not an overachiever, but solid B's.) I never did anything *really* bad. Well, that's not entirely true. I was never *caught* doing anything really bad. Be good, or be good at it, right?

I was part of the youth group at church. I was in a ton of extra-curriculars. Sure, I had the typical teenager attitude, but looking back, and considering myself pretty self-aware, I wasn't off the rails, or really a punk teenager either. I was respectful to adults, and people in general. Sure, I was *a little different*, but generally speaking, I was a good kid.

But it wasn't enough.

Mom's direction, "Prove to me that you deserve a car."

But how?

I was **so frustrated**.
And **confused**.

How, *exactly*, was I supposed to 'prove' myself to her?

Some kids received the, "get all A's and you can have ____." Or something of that sort.

Psychology calls that **positive reinforcement**.

However, I was left with absolutely no specific, tangible opportunities in which I could succeed.

Now put yourself in your partner's shoes.

They have just made one of the worst decisions of their lives. They are now acutely aware of how badly they have hurt you. And, if you have gotten to this point in your relationship, your partner is probably wanting nothing more than to make things right.

But *how*?
That's actually our part.

Without opportunities to succeed, ones that *you provide*, your partner is going to be my teenage self; going through the motions, aimlessly.

If you really are committed to moving forward with your partner, this is an absolute must. (I feel like I am starting to say that about everything.) If someone needs to earn back trust, you **must** give them the tools, and opportunity to do so. There is no point going through the motions, if you don't consciously do this.

I am not saying that it's necessary, or even possible to give someone an exact checklist to earning back someone's trust, or to give someone an ETA on how long it will take you to heal and forgive. But what you can do, is give your partner some tangible, literal things they can *do.*

Give them the tools and situations to try.
Tell them what you need from them.
*Remember what I said about expectations?

> They already fucked up, royally, so make it clear what you need from them to move forward.

Member the chapter on triggers? While arguably one of the worst parts of trauma, are also **one of the biggest opportunity for success.**

Remember the department store story?
Being open about the label gave him the opportunity to succeed with <u>how he responded</u>.

Lord knows there will be no shortage of triggers in the months and even years following an affair, so why not turn those nasty suckers into something productive.

Another one of my triggers was a Philly Cheesesteak. Silly, right? (You can continue reading when you stop laughing, it's cool.) But when we were stationed in New Jersey, getting a cheesesteak was our tradition every time we would go to the airport to pick up a family member. It was our thing. Until I saw the pictures on her Facebook that he brought 'her' there for the day to explore and try her first cheesesteak. Insert sad face.

Admitting that to him could've gone two ways.
1. He could've laughed and dismissed my feelings, calling them ridiculous, or claiming that I was finding things to be upset about.
2. He could've listened and apologized. Then he could've planned a sweet, romantic picnic in the park for us, complete with cheesesteaks and my favorite wine. Because he 'likes eating meaty sandwiches with me the best." This gesture would at least start to replace the negative memories with positive ones.

This may sound super cheesy (pun intended), or super romantic. I get it. It may seem completely frivolous out of context, but if your partner approached a situation like this in this way, I bet that the next time you thought of cheesesteak, even if those negative associations come up, they will almost certainly be silenced by the thought of that romantic picnic.

Eventually, (I swear it's true), you will start to only associate them with the picnics.

Because that's how our brains are wired.
We are meant to forget trauma.

If women really remembered how painful childbirth is, there would be far more single-child families.

OTHER OPPORTUNITIES TO SUCCEED

Do you like small gifts? Flowers? Want to be taken out on more dates? Want verbal gestures like love notes or shout-outs on social media? Whatever it is, no matter how simple or grand, if it is how you receive love, then its valid. But you have to actually tell him. <u>You cannot make them guess.</u>

**Tell them.
Be specific.**

Allow **them to succeed.**

This is where the idea of it being *an opportunity* comes in. This is where the open communication, vulnerability and trust can come back in.

Your openness *should* be rewarded.

In a healthy relationship, the reward *is* the healthy relationship.

If you are honest with your partner about what would make you feel loved and special, they should *want* to do those things for you. (Not just on Valentine's Day.)

If you are in a relationship that is healing, then the hope is, that if you are really open with your communication, your partner will hopefully run with it.

Hopefully they step up to the plate.

But of course, you have another part to play.

You have to allow it to happen.

Allow them to take you on that date. And allow yourself to enjoy it. Be in the moment. Appreciate the gesture and the time together. Allow them to take the family on a hike. (Or just them and the kids!) And allow yourself to enjoy it. (Your alone time *and* the gesture.)

11 RE-IGNITING THAT FLAME

Sex, or lack thereof, is now a reward or punishment.

Yep, you read that right.
And if you are going through anything similar to my story, you probably have mixed feelings about being intimate with your partner again.

Turns out, a lot of long relationships expierence this...

I think it's safe to assume that for most couples, intimacy stopped once the infidelity came to light. I mean, how can someone expect to be open, vulnerable, and accept pleasure if you are hurting and not trusting your partner?

The almost inevitable gap in intimacy, and how long it lasts is totally up to the couple. And how aggressively they approach their forgiveness and trust building.

While most people will need that break, this is also where things can snowball to;

---

withholding sex and intimacy is used as a form of punishment for the partner's indiscretions.

While this seems somewhat justified in the moment, it can easily turn into a power play, that when used in the future, will almost certainly lead to anger and frustration.

Since I found out about the affair only a couple weeks before I delivered our second baby, there was a mandatory 6-week break from sex. And I wasn't even considering his sexual needs after the baby was born, so there was nothing extra for him coming from me! But as I approached the end of the medical celibacy, I found myself thinking that he didn't deserve to have me intimately since with the affair he acted as though he didn't appreciate what he had.

This notion, while relatable to most, isn't really a healthy way to approach intimacy in a relationship. While it can be playful to 'reward' our partner with a sexual act, on the other hand, withholding as a form of punishment, devalues the relationship, and can only lead to greater frustration.

And since many of us are sexual beings in our own right, the lack of intimacy is not only 'punishing them' but **it's also punishing you.**

It's not exactly rocket science that sex increases intimacy and grows connections. It also releases feel-good chemicals in your brain, and it a great stress-reducer. (Okay, that is a little scientific.)

Guess what all of those things have in common?
They are all suggested ways to cope with grief.
Why withhold yourself?

For many of us, **FEAR** is a lot of what's holding you back. And it comes in so many forms when you are talking about intimacy with someone who has broken your trust.

My fear was that of rejection. Fear that I wouldn't be desirable to my husband anymore. Fear that he would be thinking of 'her' when being intimate with me. Fear that he would think he got away with his behavior and it might lead him to thinking he could get away with it again. And those are just a few of those nasty thoughts.

When you think you are ready, here are some of my thoughts on how to get started, what issues might come up, and how to get past them.

First, ask your partner out on a date.
I know, that sounds crazy. They hurt you so badly, and now I am suggesting you ask them out?

Hear me out.

Depending on the couple, you became aware of your partners infidelity weeks or months ago. And, if you have gotten to this point, where you feel like you are forgiving, and you want to truly get back to a good place, you probably have a partner that's been facing some hard truths about themselves.

The honest truth about infidelity is it is more often less about the sex (or other person), and more about the individual being deviant. Facing your demons is a humbling, exhausting, and emotionally draining process. If your partner has really been taking this seriously, then they have been walking through the fire.

One of the benefits of relationships is being able to rely on each other when we face crisis in life. But when the crisis is *in* the relationship, not only are your battling the fight, but you're basically doing it alone.

It's easy, and understandable, to view ourselves as the main 'victim' in this scenario, and we are. But trying to earn back someone's love, trust and admiration is not to be understated. It takes hard work on their part.

So, extend the olive branch. Ask them out. No pressure. No sexts necessary. And make it something meaningful. If you love the outdoors, take a hike, go to a concert, go to a dog park. Something other than just dinner. In my humble opinion, include an adult beverage. Not too many, maybe just one or two. But seriously, that one vodka martini was definitely not a bad idea.

The rest is really up to you.

For us, and our modest budget, most of our 'dates' were spending time doing things around the house; gardening, re-tiling our bathroom, cooking, etc. Sure, it wasn't exciting in the traditional sense of the word, but we both really loved d.i.y projects and 'playing house' and it got us talking and almost forced us to reconnect.

THE ONLY RULE:
Don't discuss the affair or any other difficult topics.

With that said, if you get triggered, you *should* mention it. But this isn't the time to talk about it like you would in therapy. Bring it up, but keep it short so you can move on and enjoy your time together.

Not sure how to delicately bring it up?

> "I don't want to spoil the mood, but _____ triggered me and I just had to get it off my chest. We don't have to talk about it, I just had to get it out. "

It allows you to get it out, so you aren't bottling it up. It also gives an easy way for your partner to acknowledge it without feeling like they have to dig deeper.

Now for the potential awkward ending to the date...

If you didn't drop hints that your partner may get some sexy time, then there is no pressure to end the date with intimacy. Of course, if you have a good time, and are feeling it, by all means, get down with your bad self.

But if you don't feel ready, you should have avoided any awkwardness and although your partner may be a little bummed that the date didn't lead to some intimacy, they should, at the very least, appreciate the gesture of the date, and spending some good, quality time together.

Going through this process, looking at everything that was or is 'wrong' in your relationship can really take it's toll. It's so easy to just get over the whole thing: the relationship, the working on yourselves. Especially when it's usually intimacy that makes life's bull shit easier to deal with. So, if you aren't having that, it can be especially hard.

You have to make the effort. You have to make the time for doing something else as a couple that makes you happy.

Ending with sexy time or not, you should both walk away from these dates feeling like you are moving in the right direction. And in the saga of forgiveness, you have to celebrate the little victories.

So, what about when you *do* reintroduce intimacy...

This is that really dark, in your head, super critical, bullshit part.

The mindfuck of **fear.** (This is a running theme.)

Fear of comparison.
Fear of not being enough: sexy enough, pretty enough, good enough in bed.

When society has a history of telling women, predominantly, that our men wouldn't cheat it we were pretty enough, it we were good enough wives, if we were freaky enough in the bedroom, it's damn near impossible to not have those thoughts creep in.

> Even for those of us with a decent self-confidence, the act of infidelity is a massive mindfuck of ...
>
> "I'm not worthy."

But the truth is, cheating has very little to do with any of *that*. The most gorgeous, interesting, sexy, engaging, smart, people have been cheated on. If only being beautiful were all it took! I mean, Jay Z admitted to cheating on Beyoncé. Right?

One of the biggest mindfucks for me was the feeling of <u>being out of control</u>. I wasn't able to control what he did. I wasn't able to control if he wanted to stay or not. I wasn't able to control if he wanted to leave me to be a single mother. I couldn't control my feelings. I couldn't control my living situation. I had lost control.

Bringing intimacy back into our relationship gave me back my power.

And not like I mentioned before, as holding it as a punishment or reward, but the choice to **allow myself to receive pleasure.**

That was a turning point.
It wasn't going to be about *him*.

It was going to be about me wanting to give myself pleasure. Physical pleasure in the form of an orgasm, but also pleasure in knowing that would bring back something to the relationship that was missing. I knew that would be a huge olive branch, of sorts, to my husband, because it is a sign that things are inching forward. A sort of acknowledgement of his work for all the hard work he was putting in to gain back trust.

Again, it wasn't directly a reward in the traditional sense, but it would show him that I was starting to heal, which is ultimately what our partners should be striving for.

However, that doesn't mean the *actual sex* is going to be great straight out the gate.
(I hope it is!)

A woman's mind can be a tricky place.

Below are some things that go through women's brains during sex. They can be especially loud after something traumatic has happened.

You will most likely expierence all, or most of these.

You are, almost certainly, going to worry about comparison. Do they look better naked then me? Were they more experimental in bed? I'd say this is the most common mental obstacle when it comes to bringing back intimacy after an affair.

And the only remedy I have come up with for this one is self-love, communication and time.
I fully understand that that answer is becoming annoyingly redundant...

Personally, these feelings would creep up when we were being intimate for a long time. A really long time. *Another helpful side effect of that one vodka drink.

You have to be patient. And honest. (Maybe don't be honest in the actual moment, unless of course, it is consuming you.) But if it is happening, try mentioning it to your partner afterward.

Maybe try doing it somewhere other than the bedroom, or trying a new position, or something to make it new.

We went to see 50 Shades of Grey about a year after the affair. The new bedroom stuff we tried after the movie finally replaced the thoughts of what theirs had been like.

I was no longer wondering what she did that he liked.
Instead, I was thinking about the new stuff that he and I were trying and liking.

It was another way of taking back control.

Going back to the honestly, one of the best pieces of advice I have ever gotten is to make your expectations known. Do I need to repeat that…again?
(Just re-read it.)

I don't care if this your first job, you're hiring a baby sitter, it's your 40th birthday party, or what you want for Christmas, no one will know what you want, or expect, if you don't tell them.

If you don't really know what you want, or how to articulate that to your partner, read up on the languages of love. Shoot, read about it together.

This is a great time to get verbal about your sexual needs.

Going back to my story, I had just given birth, so I already felt like a hot mess. His other woman was younger, thinner, and didn't have boobs full of milk.
I needed affirmations that he found me attractive.
Now I don't want to make him sound like a total jerk, he did pay me compliments here and there.

But his compliments were often more motherly-beautiful, and less sexual, your-my-lover beautiful.

Since he was going through the trenches of trying to win back trust and make this relationship work,

---

I should *assume* that he was attracted to me, right?

I should've been able to believe him when he occasionally told me I was beautiful, right?

I wish. But it just doesn't work like that.

If he was thinking that my bigger-than-usual booty was looking good, I needed him to say it out loud.

> Many of us need those affirmations. They need to be loud. Loud enough to drown out the negative voices in our heads.

But in *his mind*, he was worried that it would sound offensive, given the nature of what we had been going through.

Once again, communication of my expectations was the solution. It not only gave me what I needed, it gave him yet another opportunity to succeed.

It doesn't matter who you are, re-introducing intimacy into your relationship after infidelity is going to be a journey.

Hopefully, a healing one.

But the truth is, in some cases, it might not be.

In some relationships, this is going to possibly be the final straw for the relationship. You see, this period in your relationship is dealing with the foundation of an intimate relationship. Sex is what differentiates between your best friend and your lover.

How your partner approaches intimacy might reveal some clues into an unhealthy situation.

I wish I could say that everyone that follows my advice would live happily ever after. But since we all know that's bull, I wouldn't be doing my duty, if I didn't shed light on the other side.

It is entirely possible that even after you both make a decision to stay, have done therapy, and tried to re-ignite the flame, that it still isn't working.

Maybe you have communicated your expectations and they weren't received well, or maybe there just isn't any follow through. There are so many little nuances that could shift everything during this process.

My suggestion is once again, communication. Followed with good, old-fashioned go-with-your-gut.

If you give someone the tools and opportunity to succeed, and they still don't, then maybe they aren't worth the effort.

Even for couples with the best intentions, you may go through this entire process and realize that staying in this relationship isn't the best choice for you.

If ever there was a time that clarity might come to you, it's likely to come now.

12 SO... NOW WHAT?

You made it to the end of the book. Congratulations!

So, all is good.
All is forgiven!
No?

If you have made it to this point, you're awesome.
You are a decent human who gives a shit about their relationship.

You *chose* forgiveness.

> Take a quick moment to celebrate that.

No one can promise that things will work out.
But they **can work out.**

> It *is possible* to achieve forgiveness.

It is possible to have a happy, healthy, trusting relationship with your partner again.
It's not a guarantee, but it is a possibility.

When this topic comes up, especially in groups of new friends I think they are always surprised to hear that we went through this.

We are passionate, and we fight! But I think most of our friends and acquaintances would say we seem to be a really solid couple.
And we are.

I'm not so obnoxious as to say that my relationship is what everyone should be striving for.

What I *am* saying, though, is that it's possible.

Whatever your best relationship looks like, even if you didn't have it with your partner before, it's possible to have it now. Because you'll have the tools.

If you're one for analogies, your relationship is like a test. You and your partner failed before because you didn't study for it and you didn't know the subject matter. Now it's like you not only know the material, you even got the answers! Now you just have to go take the test again.

Have strength and confidence that your relationship *can* get better. You need to know this like you know you'd pass the test if you were given the answers ahead of time.

Once again, *can,* not *will.*

But happiness really is an option.
Crazy as that sounds.

Now, go!

Take this painfully logical advice and apply it to your specific situation. Take the suggestions, open your heart and ears and actually *do the work.*

Like I've mentioned before, there are also some good books on forgiveness in general. And on relationships. And on knowing how you receive love. Lord knows I am no therapist and most of this is just coming from me, a woman who has gone through this and come out the other side.

But there are *actual* professionals on these subjects. Look them up. Read them.

Treat this process with the attention it deserves.

> Forgiveness isn't for pussies.
> But it *can* come.
>
> And it's worth the fight.

ABOUT THE AUTHOR

Jules was born on the cusp of that infamous millennial generation. And while that may explain her bold, unapologetic, way of speaking her truth, (not to mention her ideals on breaking the silence and stigma attached to sexual betrayal.) But she also broke the mold of her generation by marrying and starting a family young, not to mention setting aside her Interior Design career and willingly becoming a stay-at-home parent and military wife, with 6 years of marriage, 2 children, 4 home states and one massive affair, under her belt before 30.

Better defined as a creator, Jules passion for writing crept in un-intentionally after too many conversations on relationship betrayals, as she encountered more and more couples who had silently shared the same struggle and hadn't found any guidance that helped.

She has found comfort in her walking contradiction; respecting commitment, while simultaneously working to live her strong, independent, truth. And that's how her book on infidelity reads; modern, inclusive, non-judgmental, honest and approachable. (Kind of like Jules, herself!) And coming from a family of healers and therapists, it's no real surprise that she chose to share her story, minus the bullshit,

She can be found settled (like a damn gypsy) in Southern California, still married (you know you were wondering), or on that thing known as Insta @DiscoveringTheHiddenJules

Made in the USA
Columbia, SC
02 July 2022